Iron Magnolias

A play

Barry L. Hillman

Samuel French—London
New York-Toronto-Hollywood

ISBN 0 573 13210 0

Please see page iv for further copyright information

CHARACTERS

Freda Alcutt
Daisy Locke
Evadne Sanders
Dottie Pinkerton
Bluebell Palmer
Roslyn Palmer
Doreen Small

The action of the play takes place in a hairdressing salon

Time: the present

IRON MAGNOLIAS

The interior of a smart little High-Street-type hairdressing salon in one of the low streets of a big Midlands town. The back of the setting looks out on to the street, with its double display windows and a central art nouveau door. The three remaining interior walls, including the proscenium, are lined with basins, mirrors, hairdriers and all the paraphernalia of a thriving modern salon

As the Lights come up, the shop appears empty; but presently, a few downstage gurgles draw our attention to the presence of Freda. She is an elderly, rather muddled customer, who seems unable to complete a sentence without its deterioration into a sequence of mouthed euphemisms. Her cape-encrusted shoulders are slumped over the basin and her head is buried deeply in its ceramic confines

Daisy enters briskly. She beams at the audience

Daisy Oh, hallo. Welcome to my *bijou* establishment. I call it my little beauty retreat for ladies *d'un age certaine*. Well, we mustn't let ourselves go, must we? And I must say I've done rather well for myself. Dancers among you may recall me from your visits to the local Palais de Danse. No? Well, I used to work there, in what was officially known as "a lavatorial assistance capacity"; though I liked to think of myself more as a Powder Room Attendant. Our ballroom dancing contests became quite a feature on television's *Come Dancing* programme, and it was bruited abroad that we might become a permanent familiar feature: till the hall got sold as a roller-skating rink—and I was given the elbow: well, "the golden foot-shake", you might call it! On the proceeds of which I set up this little hairdressing business. "Locks", I call it, on account of my name being Daisy Locke—Locke's. Geddit? (*She tugs meaningfully at her own coiled hair*)

Freda Gurgle, gurgle!

Daisy Oh, my God, she's drowning!

She hauls Freda's face out of the water by the scruff of her sodden neck-hairs

Freda Ouf! Ooh—er—aw...

Daisy (*loudly*) Yes, dear—lovely! I'm sure the conditioner's taken by now.

Freda (*with eyes tightly screwed*) But it's got in me what's-it, and run all down me... (*She mouths the concluding words: "bleeding face"*)

Daisy Never-you-mind-never-you-mind. We'll dab it all dry. Can't have you crying at your own wedding, can we? (*She blots heavily at the wet mess with a bulky towel*) That's a job for the bride's mother. Though Gawd knows where *she* must be by now... (*She lifts her eyes to heaven. To the audience*) That's the nice thing about this job: we keep in touch. Freda here used to be one of my ballroom ladies: olde tyme—what else...? Snowdrop polka champions nineteen sixty-seven, her and her late husband, Fred. (*She makes a sound by sharply sucking air through pursed lips*) Terrible business. Dropped dead on the dance floor. They were right in the middle of the square tango, and they'd just reached the glide-and-dip section when he collapsed in her clutch—(*she nods*) her clutch. She's a game girl though: she dragged the corpse round the floor till the end of the number, with maximum points from a judgement of three ex-valeta professionals. The judges were most impressed: just assumed he was executing a very low dip.

The front door opens with a loud bang and Evadne erupts into the salon. She is a smart, weathered woman of uncertain years, though probably over sixty. Her too-blonde hair is piled to a height of two feet in an elaborate coiffure. *Under her tent coat she is wearing a huge puff-ball creation of pink tulle*

Evadne Darling! Have I caught you?

Daisy (*to the audience; dourly*) Makes me feel like a shop-lifter in my own firm. (*Out loud, over her shoulder to Evadne*) I was hanging on special, Evadne!

Evadne takes off her coat, and the chiffon scarf that is draping her hair

(*Aside*) Another of my dance clients: Evadne Sanders. Modern Runner-Up. That's Modern, as opposed to Greek, dancing, and at total variance to Contemporary. She was Ginger Rogers' stand-in for a film version. Likes to think she's a cut above the rest of us.

Evadne I've brought the rosebuds in a Sainsbury's ice-cream container, so they won't get crushed.

Daisy Big contest tonight. (*She winks at the audience*) I sculptured the *coiffure* this morning and promised I'd insert the rosebuds after lunch.

Evadne Still attending to the blushing bride? Better get a move on. The ceremony's at four. (*She moves down stage*)

Daisy (*to the audience*) It's my Old Age Pensioners' Cheapo today. Though I advertise it as "A Senior Beauty's Discount Treatment". Evadne won't admit to the former, so I fit her in early. She still demands the full knock-down though.

Evadne (*to Freda; loudly*) I said time's getting on, dear. (*As to an imbecile*) Be late for your own funeral next.

Daisy (*admonitively*) Evie...

Freda She's been giving me a colour rinse, Evadne. Now me ears are the same colour as me hair, and there's a big brown rivulet stained right down... (*She points and mouths "me bloody cleavage"*)

Evadne It'll go lovely with the pink wedding, dear: everything's pink, isn't it? Like that there—that—oooh—that woman...

Daisy (*helpfully*) Barbara Cartland?

Evadne (*crossly*) No. That Dolly Partman in the hairdressing film. (*She titivates herself in an invisible mirror. No longer for Freda's ears*) Still, could hardly dress her in virginal white, could they? Not after Fred... (*Uncertainly*) As far as we know... Who'd have thought she'd end up with a Yank, so long after the war. She'd certainly had enough *during* it.

Daisy Now then.

Evadne He was doing his tourist bit at Cleethorpes Holiday Camp and won the Glamorous Grandad Contest. He had to do a winner's lap of honour in the Viennese Waltz section and chose Freda as a partner. (*She dabs her eyes daintily*) It's all terribly romantic. (*To Daisy.* Sotto voce) Shift the old bat along the production line, can't you, Daisy?

Freda The bridegroom was lost in Vietnam, y'know.

Evadne Couldn't find his way out of a paper bag in Chinatown, Birmingham, if you ask me.

Daisy shows disapproval

(*To Daisy*) Well, he is nearly eighty, you know.

Freda (*stricken with conscience*) Oh, do you think I ought to be marrying again at my age? (*She wails*) My Fred could be looking down in disapproval at this very moment.

Evadne and Daisy look around wildly, half expecting him to materialise from the heavens

'Cause it is tantamount to... (*She mouths "bigamy, y'know"*) Oh, will he be turning in his grave?

Evadne For a man who couldn't even turn decently on a dance floor, I shouldn't imagine that a grave would give him much scope for improvement.

Daisy (*to Freda; quickly*) I'll just re-set last week's perm lightly and pop you under the drier, dear.

She commences battle and Evadne drifts up stage

Evadne Course, she's right. How the mighty are fallen. She's exchanging glamour for domesticity. It's a wonderful world, the world of ballroom dancing, Daisy. (*She floats around*) When I step into the spotlights, dazzlingly reflected in the polished woods—it's like, it's like...

Daisy (*flatly*) Stepping back thirty years in time.

Evadne halts with pursed lips but does not respond

Evadne But it's not all sophistication, you know: people think of the glitter and the romance. They don't realise the hell we go through: the talcum up one's nose; the million shreds off boas drifting down one's throat; the lacquer glueing one's eyelids together (*through a grimly stolid jaw*) and Neville Coggins squeezing his spots in the communal mirror before slapping on his Boots Man-Tan... (*She starts at the window*) Good God— talking of which, here's Neville's putative mother-in-law— Roslyn's mum: as pig-ignorant as her daughter and a typical Midlander—incapable of agreeing with a single statement made to her, either in the case of political polemics or in the

lightest civilities of social badinage. She looks like the Grim
Reaper in that wedding tackle.

*Bluebell Palmer explodes into the shop with a face that would
have done the late Les Dawson proud*

(*She goes to greet her*) Darling, you look wonderful!
Bluebell My Roslyn's in a hell of a mess!

Evadne lays a swift attenuated hand on the woman's forearm

Evadne Thank *God* everything's normal.
Bluebell (*advancing*) I warned her she should never have agreed
to be Freda's chief bridesmaid.
Evadne Bluebell—to *think* if Neville Coggins had only done the
right thing by her, she could have been *Matron of Honour*!
What a pity he ran off with that young man from the Penge
Formation Team.
Bluebell I told her she'd do no good with that one, with his dyed
blond hair and his nipped-in waist line. (*She fixes Evadne as
would a basilisk*) I thought it was *you* coming in first time I
saw him.
Evadne And his skin-tight panties so high you could hang a hat
on his crotch. (*She shudders*) "Ballroom" was an expression he
never could come to terms with.
Bluebell She's given up men now. Taken to gardening.
Daisy (*to the audience*) The nearest Roslyn ever got to gardening
was when Clay Jones's dog shat on her lawn. (*To Bluebell*)
Well, whatever ails the girl, Bluebell?
Bluebell It's those ringlet things you did for her, to go with her
head-dress. Losing all their screw they are.
Daisy Oh, dear. (*In all seriousness*) It's not like Roslyn to lose
a good screw.

Evadne looks at the audience with a beseeching helplessness, as if to say "to comment further would be bootless"

Bluebell Could you give 'em a tightening, if she pops in?

Daisy Of course, love: though strictly speaking it *is* Pensioners' Day.

Evadne Oh, surely not *all* day, dear? (*She smiles weakly*)

Bluebell (*to Freda as to a child*) No first-night nerves, Freda?

Freda shakes her head and smiles inanely

(*To the others*) Her water-works are all to pot, you know.

Evadne You don't have to tell *me*, darling. I think they'll have to give her a kidney transplant *after* she's dead. They used to dance right off stage and into the dressing-room after a Dinky One-Step bout. The judges thought it very novel. But *we* all knew it was first stop the Penny Peep Show for that pair. (*She rises and addresses Freda*) I'll be at the church, dear. But I'll keep my coat on. Don't want to steal the limelight on your special day, do I? I'll not stay to the reception, though. Not for Frogetts' Sit-Down teas. Their battered cod always looks like it's been mugged as well.

Bluebell Who's giving you away, dear?

Freda That nice Mr Bellamy from the Old People's Home, I think... (*She mouths "he's the warder"*)

Bluebell I think she means he's the *warden*, Daisy.

Evadne Oh, dear. Will there be room for his Zimmer frame?

Bluebell I daren't ask who's going to be the best man.

Evadne Probably the vicar, judging from the rest of the cast-list. I mean, *guest*-list. I do hope he omits his usual helpful hints on family planning this time.

The door pings open and Dottie Pinkerton sails in. She is big,

*busty and hearty. Although as horsey as her daughter Valerie,
she lacks her offspring's reticence and calls a spade a spade*

Dottie Hallo, girls! Dishing the dirt?

Daisy (*apprehensively*) Dottie! I hope you haven't come for a
hair-do. It's appointments only on Senior Citizens' Day.

Bluebell and Evadne join her

Dottie (*plonking herself astride a chair*) Oh, don't worry about
me, old girl. I think I can still make something out of that trim
you gave me last year. No, I only slipped in to buy some slap.
Valerie says I ought to make an effort with the old pancake—
being as it's a special do. All a load of malarkey, if you ask me.

Daisy (*leaving Freda to go and rootle in the cosmetics display*)
What sort of thing were you thinking about, Dottie?

Dottie Well, what about a nice pink blusher to stipple over the
old red veins, eh?

Bluebell O-ooh, I'm not sure pink blusher will mix well with
tweeds, Dottie.

Dottie Oh, don't be daft, Bluebell. I shan't be wearing tweeds at
a wedding! No—I've got a nice corduroy suit that'll be ideal.

Evadne They do say that plum-coloured lipsticks are coming
back in.

Dottie (*getting up*) Trust you to know all the bloody *fol-de-rols*.
I've heard of mutton dressed up as lamb, but in your case it's
more like a dead sheep!

Evadne (sotto voce) Charming.

Dottie And what have you got yourself up as now? Have you
fallen off a Christmas tree, or are you acting as unofficial
bridesmaid, on leave from the local Gilbert and Sullivan
society?

Evadne (*starchly*) I'm competing in the national dance trophy after the happy event. Anyway, your Valerie could have been partnering Bluebell's Roslyn as a bridesmaid—if she hadn't got herself in that—interesting situation.

Freda nods wildly to the others, smugly pointing to her stomach, miming that Valerie is pregnant, and mutely mouthing "she's pregnant, y'know"

Dottie You mean on account of her being in the family way?

Evadne I mean in the event of her having to leave the library in dubious circumstances.

Dottie Narrow-minded bunch of local government officials! You can't expect a girl to work part-time at a stud farm and not get a few ideas of her own.

Evadne (*only just to herself*) God help the horses.

Dottie Anyway, she's always preferred the stables routine. She's going to be something big with Captain Mark Phillips's team.

Evadne Yes, and getting bigger by the day, I shouldn't wonder.

Daisy Is she going to attend the wedding, Dottie?

Dottie Feels a bit coy about it; but I said she could wear one of my old trench coats.

Bluebell Oh, I don't think she ought to go in a church in *that* condition, Dottie.

Dottie Why not? It's a perfectly good trench coat.

Bluebell No. I mean—being up the spout.

Freda nods vigorously and mimes "Up the spout! Up the spout!"

Dottie Well, with most of the brides in the same shape, I don't see why she shouldn't.

Freda *I'm* not in the... (*She mouths "same shape!"*)

Daisy (*hastily returning to the rescue with an armful of products*) Look, I've got a whole range of samples here, Dottie. Why don't you just amuse yourself trying some of them out in the mirror there? (*She points* R)

Dottie (*accepting*) Course, I've always known she was far too naïve. It's always the innocent ones who end up in the pudding club. Spent a lifetime at that library handing out books by Marie Stopes, and still thinks a Dutch cap is an item of costume from *Miss Hook of Holland*. Now, if it had been your Roslyn——

Bluebell What do you mean?

Dottie Far too fly to get caught.

Evadne (*bright-eyed and bushy-tailed*) Oh, she's taken up gardening now instead.

Dottie Gardening! The nearest Roslyn ever got to gardening was when Clay Jones's dog shat on her lawn.

Daisy (*over-hastily*) Yes, well, that's quite enough of *that* sort of talk in *my* salon.

Dottie (*twisting round whilst dabbing an inordinate amount of blue eye-shadow on one lowered lid*) Oh, look—talk of the devil—there's your Roslyn now; and in her bridesmaid frock. Looks like a pink sofa on legs.

Bluebell Well!

Roslyn leaps in and stands panting against the slammed door

Roslyn Oh, just look at me, Daisy! I'm all unscrewed.

Evadne (*athletically retouching a false eyelash*) Not what *I've* just heard, darling!

Freda Ooh, I don't think you ought to be seen in public wearing all your—(*she mouths "wedding tackle"*)—Roslyn! It's terrible bad luck, y'know.

Roslyn (*darting to Freda's elbow*) Not for *me*, it isn't. For you, for *you*, y'daft old bat!

Bluebell Now, Roslyn, don't get her excited. If she wets her drawers, I'll never forgive you.

Roslyn Oh, I wish I'd never agreed to all this.

Evadne (*falsely helpful*) Now don't you worry about looking like a sofa, dear: I'm sure all that puffiness will look *splendid* once in the appropriate setting.

Roslyn Pardon?

Dottie And anyhow, I hear you're to be the new Daphne Ledward! (*She now has her other eyelid bright green*)

Roslyn Eh?

Dottie Taking over in the revamped radio edition of *Gardeners' Question Time*.

Roslyn What are you on about?

Evadne We've been hearing about your new horticultural bent. You mother's been telling us about your Love-Lies-Bleeding.

Roslyn What about it?

Evadne How it bled to death!

They collapse in laughter, Dottie splodging rouge on one of her cheeks

Roslyn I think you've all gone barmy!

Daisy (*taking charge*) Well, don't let 'em get you in a flap, Roslyn. You just help me shift Freda over to the drier, and then you can slip into her chair and I'll see to you.

They carry Freda by the elbows L, *where a hood hairdrier awaits them*

Freda (*bewildered*) Where are you taking——

Daisy We're just going to pop you under the drier, dear.

Freda Oh, I hope it won't take too long. I don't want to keep Beau waiting...

Evadne For God's sake, he's been waiting eighty years. A few more minutes shouldn't hurt.

Freda He does tend to… (*She mouths "get his hair off"*)
Evadne That shouldn't be a lengthy process these days.

They settle Freda in the chair and lower the hood over her

Roslyn (*in her ear; loudly*) Have you been?
Freda What? Oh, yes. I'm fine. There's nothing wrong. (*She points in a southerly direction and plainly mouths "with my bladder!"*)
Roslyn (*returning to the group*) Honestly, it's obscene. What on earth are they going to *do* on their wedding night?
Evadne (*archly*) Same as you've been doing for years on your practice runs, I should think. All passions don't die just because one's over—fifty.
Roslyn (*wide-eyed*) You mean you and Cyril are still at it?
Evadne (*nostrils hardening*) Don't be coarse. My Cyril's a councillor. His thoughts are on a higher plane. He adores me, aesthetically.
Roslyn Oh. The old prostate trouble, eh? (*She plonks herself down in Freda's vacated chair*) Gawd—these sleeves *are* a bit puffy. (*She peers in the mirror*)
Evadne I'd have thought you'd have had enough of puffs after Neville.
Roslyn Yeah, well he didn't need teaching the Gay Gordons, that's for sure.
Dottie Nature will out. You should see my dogs performing. Gender's the last thing on their mind.

Evadne throws another of her mute appeals to the audience

Bluebell Oh, I don't think that sort of thing's right, Dottie. It's like Sodom and Gonorrhoea.
Dottie (*leaning over, her remaining cheek now in striking*

contrast to the first) Look, you've got to take advantage of men's weaknesses, Bluebell. Old Mr Petty next door has been courting me on and off for the last thirty years. When I find cow manure round my roses, I don't have to search for the source—Mr Petty.

Evadne (*after a pause*) I'd have thought he'd have had a little help from the cows.

Dottie These things aren't to be mocked, Evadne. When a woman of Freda's age gets married, one's feelings are heightened by the proximity of death.

Roslyn Make hay while the sun shines.

Dottie Precisely.

Evadne Hay-stacks, in *your* case.

Bluebell I don't like anything morbid.

Freda (*calling across*) Daisy!

Daisy Yes, dear?

Freda P'r'aps I *had* just better—er...

Daisy Oh, dear. She does want to go, after all. Could you see to her, Roslyn, while I prepare your hair lotions?

Roslyn (*rising and going over to Freda*) Come on, old girl. Time for the Ladies' Excuse Me!

She hauls Freda out of her seat and holds her in a dance-partner position

All set? Here we go.

They dance with surprising expertise

"Twinkle-twinkle, little tinkle". Slow-slow—quick-quick-quick-quick-quick...

They exit L

The front door pings open and Doreen walks in. She is in her late forties and has a hard, thin face; but she has a trim figure, currently wrapped in a smart but shabby belted raincoat. She has a triangular headscarf over her hair. Her voice is culti-vated and her carriage shows confidence

Doreen Is this Daisy Locke's place?

Daisy That's what it says over the doorway, dear. But I'm afraid we're fully booked at the moment.

Doreen I'm not acquainted with these downtown small busi-nesses, and I certainly wouldn't frequent one.

Daisy (*bristling*) Oh, I thought you looked in urgent need of attention.

Doreen I've no need of ordinary hairdressers. I have a private perruquier.

No response

A wig-maker.

Bluebell Are you bald, dear?

Doreen No, I'm a professional.

Bluebell (*misunderstanding*) Oh, I don't know as I hold with that——

Daisy So, how can I help you, madam?

Doreen Well, an elderly gentleman has just got out of a taxi and asked me to call in here and speak to his wife. He sounded American.

Daisy That'll be Freda. His wife-to-be, actually.

Doreen Yes, probably. So where is she?

Daisy She's—she's just arranging her *toilette* at the moment. Can I take a message?

Doreen I'm to tell her the taxi has called too early, and he's going to have to ride round and round the block till "nearer the

time"—whatever *that* means. So he'd naturally appreciate it if
she could be as quick as possible.

Dottie God, she'll get in a frightful stew if we try to rush her.

Doreen Well, that's neither here nor there. I've done my duty.
(*She turns to go*)

Evadne (*squinting*) Excuse me, but haven't I seen you before?

Doreen (*flattered*) Possibly. I'm on the box a lot.

Evadne (*pleasantly*) You deliver speeches at Hyde Park Corner?

Doreen No. I appear on television.

Bluebell Would *I* have seen you?

Doreen No. It would be past your bed-time at the rest home, dear.

Dottie So——

Doreen (*snootily*) I'm a professional dancer. I do the speciality
solos in the *Come Dancing* programmes.

Evadne (*rising to her full height*) I knew it! I was sure I'd seen
that sneer before! It's Doreen Small, isn't it?

Doreen Conchita Alvara, if you don't mind. I prefer my professional sobriquet.

Evadne I bet you do! (*She addresses the crowd*) I've met this one
before, darlings. I shared a dressing-room with her. It was sheer
bloody hell.

Doreen (*defensively*) They should never have put me in with you
amateurs. I deserved a dressing-room of my own.

Evadne And you'd have bloody well *got* one, if we'd had our
way: *and* another for your ego.

Doreen I deserved a padded cell after an evening with you lot.

Dottie (*rising*) Could you please tell me what on earth is going on?

*Roslyn enters with Freda and immediately recognises the
visitor. She screams and slaps her hands over Freda's eyes*

Freda (*blinded*) Who is it? Who is it?

Roslyn You don't want to know, dear. It's an omen from the past.

Bluebell Do you know this lady, too, then, air* Ross?

Roslyn Know her! I should think I do—the woman who blighted our careers! Every syllable is etched on my memory! Know her, know her?!

Bluebell Who is it then, dear?

Roslyn I can't remember.

Her hands fall from Freda's eyes

Freda (*gasping*) Tooh-erh! It's Alohita Convara! No. Convata Alchira. No—Chitvara Conalchi. No—Con——

Roslyn (*breaking in*) It's Doreen bloody Small, that's who it pigging is.

Freda She was almost the death of my poor Fred… (*She blabs*)

Evadne (*incensed*) *Almost?* He *is* dead, isn't he?

Roslyn sits Freda down and thumps the hood of the drier down as far as her chin

Roslyn Pay no attention to her, Freda. She's obviously come to spoil your big day, just as she ruined ours. Tell it like it was, Evadne.

Evadne (*dramatically*) It was the night of the Amateur Dancing Championships, and this woman was insinuated into our company, obviously planted by our rival contestants, to undermine our competitive morale. She goaded us into performing badly by playing on our nerves.

Doreen (*open-eyed*) What are you talking about? If I remember rightly, it was *you* who tried to sabotage my number, by altering my music and bribing the band. Naturally I rose above such tactics and turned the situation to my advantage by sheer professionalism.

* (Midlands dialect for "our")

Roslyn Hogwash! You'd always been such a rubbish act the public assumed that the mistakes you made must have been improvements.

Doreen Daisy—are you going to stand idly by and condone this injustice?

Daisy Then, as now, I endeavour to remain impartial. I do recall some kind of hiatus, but the customer is always right.

Doreen I see. Honour among thieves, eh? It's an obvious example of how the solidarity of the mean-minded contributes to their lowly place in society, whereas I have risen to my present position due to my ability to accept challenges.

Evadne Your present position? And pray what is that? I don't see you providing many exhibition spots these days.

Doreen Naturally one matures. I'm more of a panellist these days.

Evadne I would have thought there were enough panel-beaters in the car industry.

Doreen A *television* panellist. I'm the guest celebrity on quiz shows.

Evadne Oh. They try to guess who the hell you are, do they?

Doreen Look, I really can't demean myself squabbling with elderly no-hopers well past their sell-by date. I've delivered my message and now I have to go. I've done my good turn for the day. (*She turns to go*)

Evadne Indeed? Might one enquire as to whether we know the gentleman?

Doreen turns back and surveys them with haughty condescension

Doreen I have an important engagement at the Croydon Embassy Ballroom.

Evadne (*now unsure*) For the Penge versus Anerley Finals?

Doreen Yes.

Evadne But that's where *I'm* competing tonight.

Doreen How exciting for you. I'll wish you good luck. You'll need it: I'm one of the judges.

She turns towards the door, catches sight of Dottie's painted face and, holding it by the chin, examines it

You'll have to run very hard to catch up with your friends, dear. The circus left town yesterday.

She exits

Stunned silence

Roslyn There you are, you see. The Wicked Witch of the West, out to make mischief and succeeding admirably.

Dottie Still, it was kind of her to deliver Beau's message.

Roslyn sits and Daisy starts to twist and clamp her errant locks

Bluebell She ought never to have wished you good luck, Evadne. It's bad luck to wish theatricals good luck. She should have said "Break a leg."

Dottie She was probably being considerate—knowing how many women of your age already have a marked propensity towards leg breaking.

Evadne You mean as opposed to women of your own type, (*now thoroughly unladylike*) who tend to be discovered with their teeth kicked in?

Roslyn You see? Señora Alvara is already getting us at logger-heads again.

Daisy Oughtn't we to let Freda know of Beau's predicament, before the poor man gets giddy circling the block?

Roslyn (*jumping up, hair clamps jangling*) Oh, I've left her in overdrive. She'll be baked to a frazzle.

Evadne (*going over with Roslyn*) Come along, Freda. That man of yours is getting impatient. The impetuosity of youth!
Dottie (*dancing over, singing raucously*) "There was he,
                    waiting at the church,
                    waiting at the church,
                    wait——"

A sudden silence

Bluebell She's very quiet.
Roslyn Here, give me a hand unscrewing this hood off her head.

Daisy trips over. They tug and twist

Daisy She's awfully red; I might almost say—singed.

A momentary pause while they contemplate the apparition, then fall to their task with redoubled alacrity

Evadne Are you all right, dear? Just a little flushed? (*She taps at the encarnadined features*)—She's not responding. I think she's fainted.
Roslyn Water!

Bluebell dashes a glass of water in Freda's face

Don't overdo it! You're not launching the *Queen Mary*!

She interposes her own face and gets Bluebell's next contribution full in the mouth

Oud! Stop it, y'silly moo. You'll drench the lot of us.
Daisy She's not breathing.
Dottie (*looming over the entire tableau*) Here—let me get at her heart.

*She joins her fists into a sledgehammer and starts thumping
Freda's chest from above the group. Once again, Roslyn tries to
intercept the assault*

Roslyn Lay off her, will you? She might just as well die of a heart
attack as a smashed rib cage.

Bluebell It's manslaughter.

Evadne (*appalled*) I'm afraid it's worse than that. It's murder.
She's dead.

*Aghast, the dishevelled women form a silent halo round the inert
Freda*

Roslyn (*breaking the spell*) She can't be! Freda! Freda—wake
up! (*She shakes the body like a rag doll*)

Dottie (*smugly*) Now, who's breaking her rib cage?

Bluebell Oh, air Ross—you've killed her!

Roslyn It was an accident. I'll swing for that Doreen Small,
upsetting her like this.

Bluebell You'll swing anyway, love. (*She shakes her head*)

Evadne (*dabbing her eyes discreetly*) She was so happy. It was
to be a beautiful ceremony. I fully approved.

Daisy She'd got the service all worked out—beautiful music:
Mendelssohn, Wagner, Ravel…

Bluebell (*nodding doefully*) I was looking forward to hearing the
Ravel.

Evadne (*rounding on her with manic irritation*) Oh, don't be
ridiculous, Bluebell! Nobody ever looked forward to hearing
Ravel!

Daisy I shall have to cancel your hairstyle now, Evadne.

Evadne Oh, I don't see why…?

They look at her disapprovingly

Well—I shall want to look my best for the funeral, shan't I?

Dottie (*like a basilisk*) Somebody is going to have to phone for an ambulance.

Daisy The police——

Roslyn Arrrgh. I didn't do it! I didn't mean it.

Bluebell You'd better do it, Evadne. You've always had friends in low places.

They advance on the phone in a group, and stand around it in a silent circle, like nuns round an altar. Once, twice, Evadne raises a trembling hand, only to withdraw it at the last moment. The tension mounts. Suddenly a loud ring from the phone itself has them leaping backwards with a concerted shriek

Daisy (*bravely lifting the receiver*) Daisy Locke's Beauty Emporium. How may I help you? Permanents, tints, facials… Oh, yes. Yes, of course. I understand… I'll do my best, dear. Please accept my heartiest congratulations. (*She replaces the receiver*)

Evadne Well?

Daisy It was Beau. The taxi man made him get out of the car and now he's pacing about the vestry demanding that Freda joins him immediately.

Bluebell What on earth are we going to do?

Roslyn What are we going to say to him?

Evadne It'll kill him. I always said what a perfect, youthful match he was for Freda. The plucky war hero, and the skilful terpsichorean artiste.

Dottie (*knuckle to lip in thought*) It might be a good idea to get him to book the vicar for the requiem whilst he's there…

Daisy (*bristling*) How could you let something like this happen in my new shop? People will never want to come here again.

Roslyn And if you mess up their ringlets like you did mine, who can blame them?

Bluebell It'd be like entering a morgue. "The Shop of Death".

Evadne Do you think we ought to collect for a wreath? Among the regulars, I mean?

Daisy You're ghouls, ghouls! Never a thought for me. Building up an entrepreneurial business in these recessionary times— only to see it all blown away with your silly murder games.

Bluebell It was an accident. Didn't I always say it was mis-adventure?

Dottie (*booming*) You realise, of course, there'll be a jolly old inquest? You'll all be regarded as witnesses, accessories? There could even be a court case, a trial.

They all shriek

Roslyn Couldn't we hide the body and say that she left hours ago? (*In discomfort*) Well, it could save unpleasantness, and it might be kinder for the bridegroom, never knowing *quite* what her awful fate was.

Daisy Hide her? Hide her? Where could I possibly conceal her here?

Roslyn Well, you must have bin-liners.

Evadne Look, I'm going to phone the hospital. We could say we're not quite sure whether she's dead or not. Then it can be assumed that she died on the way to the surgery. That would let Daisy off the hook.

Bluebell (*sobbing*) Oh, poor Freda. She's probably dancing on the clouds right now.

Evadne (*pragmatically*) No, dear. I can't hear any great clump-ing thunderbolts yet.

Dottie Somebody will have to get down to the church.

Roslyn Well, *I* can't go, dressed like this. It's not appropriate.

Dottie We could all be arrested, you know. (*She nods sagely*)

Evadne But—but *I* can't be subjected to that. I'm due at an important function at eight.

Bluebell And I'm only here on an errand. I've got my husband's tea to get.

Roslyn And I'm going to a wedding!

Daisy (*chewing her lip and raising her hands*) Perhaps we could say she'd had a change of heart. Tell the police she couldn't go through with it, and then discover her later in the toilet; so we could say she'd probably suffered a seizure there, and that none of it actually occurred in our presence.

Bluebell But that would be perjury.

Roslyn Oh, stop raising objections, Mum. You don't want to see me on Death Row, do you?

Bluebell I didn't want to see you in that hideous dress——

Roslyn Well, then, we must all do what's best for us, and Daisy, of course. It was all an unfortunate mishap. We don't want to have it looking like a scandal.

Dottie Come on, then; let's haul her into the lavatory. It'll be an appropriate end for her.

They gather round the corpse

Bluebell Oh, I can't look.

They drop a pink towel over Freda's face

Daisy She always loved pink.

They attempt to lift her

Evadne Crikey, she's heavy! Thank God I never had to dance with her.

The door pings. They scream, and guiltily screen the chair in a semicircle

Doreen enters, looking strangely abashed

Doreen I'm sorry to intrude on you again, ladies, but…

Daisy But what?

Doreen There's been a terrible accident.

Bluebell Argh! How did you know?

Roslyn Mum—shut up!

Evadne (*sneering*) Oh? Did someone mistake you for a television star?

Doreen I walked past the church to get back to my hotel, where I have to pick up my suitcase and join the limousine for tonight's journey and I thought I'd call in and reassure the old gent that his friend was coming as quickly as she could.

Dottie She wasn't his friend. She was his wife-to-be. They were due at church to be married.

Doreen (*astonished*) Married? Those two geriatrics were getting married? Why, it's disgusting.

Roslyn (*emotionally*) Oh no, it's not! All passions don't die just because you're over fifty, y'know. And *you* would know! Emotions can be on a, on a…

Evadne A higher plane.

Roslyn Yes. A hired aeroplane.

Doreen The point is… Look. She isn't around at the moment, is she?

Roslyn ⎫ (*together*) ⎧ No!
Bluebell ⎭   ⎩ Yes.

Pause

Roslyn ⎫ (*together*) ⎧ Yes!
Bluebell ⎭   ⎩ No.

Doreen I suppose she's just popped out *to visit Auntie* yet again?

Daisy She can't hear you at any rate.

Doreen The thing is; I noticed this crowd around the building. Nothing strange in that, of course, at a church, but then the ambulance came wailing round the corner——

Dottie Well, spit it out, woman!

Doreen It appears the taxi man had felt guilty about dumping his passenger and drove back to apologise. Meanwhile the old boy was so irate by now that he stormed impatiently into the road, and the taxi man ran him down!

Bluebell Oh, no!

Pause

Daisy Is he badly hurt?

Doreen Not any more. He's dead.

Pause

Evadne (*loudly*) Well, thank God for that!

Doreen (*bewildered*) Thank God? What do you mean?

Evadne We won't have to tell him about Freda now.

Doreen Tell him what about Freda?

Roslyn (*wildly*) That she'll be late!

Daisy *Very* late.

Evadne Oh, to hell with it! She *is* late: *the* late!

Doreen (*advancing as the quartet starts to break up*) What have you done to her?

Roslyn It wasn't me! (*Hysterically*) I wasn't here!

Bluebell (*hanging on to Doreen*) Oh, don't send her to gaol! It was an accident.

Doreen What was? (*She stares down at the body*) Oh, good heavens. You've killed the poor woman.

Roslyn (*defiantly*) No, we didn't. It was you. The shock of seeing you again brought on a heart attack.

Bluebell It brought back the shame. And the pain—and poor Fred. And she's dead.

Evadne (*detaching herself from the group*) The truth of the matter is, they were both too old for such an escapade. Their constitutions weren't strong enough to survive these rigorous changes. It's all for the best. I always said it would never work out.

Doreen My God. They're both dead.

Evadne Yes. It's all rather romantic, really. They couldn't live without each other and must have spiritually decided on a mutual extinction. It's like Romeo and Juliet.

Dottie Or Tristan and Isolde.

Bluebell Or Marks and Spencer.

Evadne The plain fact is—*Conchita*, that you and I can't afford to get mixed up in this tragic affair. We're both women of an artistic calling and have our public to consider. The show must go on. *Life* must go on.

Bluebell Evadne, how can you be so callous?

Doreen (*walking over to join her*) Evadne, you're perfectly right. If the authorities get involved in this—as they undoubtedly must, our reputations would be inevitably compromised. There's bound to be speculation as to how blame should be apportioned.

Evadne (*as they stand united*) Besides which, if the bobbies once get their flat feet in here, we could be detained indefinitely— might never get to the function at all.

Doreen Precisely. And the cameras are due in.

Evadne We're obviously sympathetic, and Freda *was* my dearest friend, but these things do happen and can't be allowed to inconvenience more people than is absolutely essential.

Daisy That's a very cynical way of viewing the situation.

Evadne Of course it's cynical. The truth usually is.

An impasse

Freda (*suddenly*) Orrgh!—What's going on?

They draw back and gasp in horror. Freda looks up at Daisy and feels tentatively at her hair

    Am I done yet, dear?
Daisy Obviously *not*!
Dottie You're alive, old thing?
Freda Well, of course I am. Though I must confess I feel a bit…
    (*She mouths the word "knackered"*) So where's Beau if he's
    supposed to be collecting me?

Silence

    Will somebody kindly tell me what's happened to Beau?

They stare at one another, appalled at the fresh prospect and are still speechless as the Lights fade and——

                    —the CURTAIN *descends*

FURNITURE AND PROPERTY LIST

Further dressing may be added at the director's discretion

On stage: Washbasins
Mirrors
Hairdriers
Towels, including a pink one
Cosmetics display with make-up samples
Chairs
Glass
Phone

LIGHTING PLOT

Property fittings required: nil
Interior. The same throughout

To open: Bring up general lighting

Cue 1	They stare at one another, speechless *Fade lights*	(Page 27)

EFFECTS PLOT